Jonathan Woolf Architects

Editorial

Dieser Band erscheint gleichzeitig mit jenem zu Tony Fretton Architects. Das mag daran liegen, dass die zwei ungleichalten Architekten befreundet sind und vielleicht ebenso, dass sie nicht Konkurrenten sind, sondern Weggefährten mit einer ähnlichen architektonischen Ausrichtung. Zu dieser Ausrichtung gehört ein deutlich erkennbares Gefühl der Empathie. Der Begriff meint vorerst die Fähigkeit, sich in andere zu versetzen. Beim Architekten kann das heissen, sich in die Auftraggeber, in die Bewohner und Benützer zu versetzen, aber auch – in einer erweiterten Ebene – sich in die architektonische und städtebauliche Ausgangslage und Umgebung einfühlen, um daraus den Entwurf, die architektonischen Ideen zu entwickeln und zu nähren. Es ist gleichsam der «Stoff», aus dem die Geschichte entsteht. Diese Haltung bedingt eine grundlegende Bescheidenheit. Der Architekt gibt sich und sein Vorwissen vorerst gänzlich auf. Erst diese «Leere» lässt die Inspiration zu, um im besten Fall ein bestimmtes Mass an Freiheit oder Verfügbarkeit der Sinne zu erreichen und in diesem Zustand schliesslich den «Stoff» in ein architektonisches Konzept zu transformieren.

Hier beginnt bei Jonathan Woolf der Entwurf, der eng an den Bewohnern, Nutzungen und an den ortsspezifischen und konstruktiven Gegebenheiten liegt. Die Architektur spielt sich nicht mehr auf einer getrennten «autonomen» Ebene ab, sie ist vielfältig mit dem Leben verwoben. Die Absicht gleicht vielleicht jener in der Malerei wie sie Paul Valéry beschreibt: «Die Malerei spielt mit einem subtilen Zusammenklang der Ähnlichkeit der Dinge». So reflektiert beispielsweise der mit einem Umbau neugeschaffene komplexe Organismus eines Doppelhauses mit den vielschichtigen Verbindungen zwischen den zwei Häusern den speziellen Status der Bauherrschaft, einer zu einer 11-köpfigen Wohngemeinschaft erweiterten Familie.

Diese engen Bezüge zwischen der Ausgangslage und dem Entwurf können an den hier vorgestellten Bauten nachvollzogen werden. Die Art der Darstellung schliesslich widerspiegelt in sympathischer Art die konzentrierte und sorgfältige architektonische Handschrift Jonathan Woolfs.

Luzern, im Juni 2010 Heinz Wirz

Editorial

This volume is appearing simultaneously with the publication on Tony Fretton Architects. That may be because despite their age difference, the two architects are friends. Or equally because instead of being rivals, they are more like companions with a similar architectural approach, one that includes a clearly detectable sense of empathy. The term primarily means the ability to put oneself into the position of others. For architects, it can mean putting oneself in the position of the contractor and the building's users, but also – on an extended level – feeling one's way into the existing architectural and urban planning situation and environment in order to develop and inspire architectural ideas. It is the "stuff" from which history is made. The attitude requires an underlying degree of humility. First, the architect entirely releases himself from his own identity and previous experience. Such "emptiness" is essential for inspiration that ideally leads to a degree of freedom or availability of the senses. Ultimately it allows the above-mentioned "stuff" to be transformed into an architectural concept.

For Jonathan Woolf, this is where a design begins, close to the residents, users, the specific locations and their constructive conditions. Architecture no longer acts on a separate, "autonomous" level. It is intertwined with life. Perhaps the intention is similar to what the artist Paul Valéry described: "Painting plays on the subtle harmony of the similarity of things." In this way, the complex organism of a double building that has been newly created by an extension, with different connections between the two buildings, reflects the special status of the developer, an extended family that lives together in an 11-person community.

Such close relationships between the initial situation and the design are clearly visible in the buildings presented in this volume. The way they are presented also attractively reflects the focused, careful architectural hallmark of Jonathan Woolf.

Lucerne, June 2010 Heinz Wirz

De aedibus international

**Jonathan Woolf Architects
London**

Quart Verlag Luzern

Jonathan Woolf Architects
4. Band der Reihe De aedibus international/Volume 4 of the series De aedibus international

Herausgeber/Edited by: Heinz Wirz, Luzern
Konzept/Concept: Jonathan Woolf Architects/Mirjam Nymalm, London; Heinz Wirz
Textbeitrag/Contribution: Irina Davidovici, London
Objekttexte/Describtion of the projects: Jonathan Woolf Architects
Vorwort/Foreword: Heinz Wirz
Nachwort/Afterword: Valerio Olgiati, Flims CH
Übersetzung aus dem Englischen/Translation from the English: Thorsten Wiskamp, Gransee D
Übersetzung aus dem Deutschen (Editorial)/English Translation (Editorial): Benjamin Liebelt, Berlin
Fotos/Photos: Hélène Binet S./p. 9,13, 17, 25-31, 39-43, 49-51, 53-55, 60 (top left); Etienne Clement S./p. 57 (top right); Peter Cook S./p. 56 (bottom right), 57 (top left); David Grandorge S./p. 15-16, 48, 59 (top left); Chris Howgate S./p. 61; Neil Lamb S./p. 8 (left) 58 (top right); Ioanna Marinescu S./p. 33-37; Donnie Ross S./p. 8 (right); Matthew Weinreb S./p. 56 (top left); All other photos and images by the architects
Grafische Umsetzung/Graphic Design: Quart Verlag, Luzern
Lithos: Printeria, Luzern
Druck/Printing: Engelberger Druck AG, Stans

© Copyright 2010
Quart Verlag Luzern, Heinz Wirz
Alle Rechte vorbehalten/All rights reserved
ISBN 978-3-03761-027-5

Quart Verlag GmbH
Denkmalstrasse 2, CH-6006 Luzern
books@quart.ch, www.quart.ch

Printed in Switzerland

6	Eine literarische Architektur, Irina Davidovici/ A literary architecture, Irina Davidovici
12	Painted House, London
18	Stadtbibliothek/City Library, Stockholm
24	Brick Leaf House, London
32	Monkey Puzzle Pavilion, Aberdeen
38	Pocket House, London
44	Universitätsgebäude/University Buildings, Rapperswil
48	The Lion Rooms, London
52	Swinton Street Studios, London
56	Werkverzeichnis/List of Works
61	Biografie/Biography
62	Postskriptum, Valerio Olgiati/Postscript, Valerio Olgiati

A literary architecture
Irina Davidovici*

*To what, then, could I have aspired in my craft?
Certainly to small things, having seen that the possibility of great ones was historically precluded.*
Aldo Rossi

For some architects the most immediate source of inspiration is not internal – personal creativity – but external: the world. Jonathan Woolf's architecture has the kind of openness that is characteristic of this condition. It doesn't impose, it responds. Originality manifests itself through the unexpected juxtaposition of elements, or fragments, that are normally unrelated. In a word – wit, if wit was understood not as mere conversational skill but in the more profound sense, as the capacity to reveal the hidden relationships between distant phenomena.

The openness of this work leads to an avoidance of stylistic constants, the rejection of a recognizable formal sensibility being a priori imposed on a situation. The projects only resemble each other inasmuch as their circumstances are similar; and circumstances, thankfully, inevitably, vary.

In the context of this publication, the sense of openness and response to context will be taken almost as a given. Much of the recent Swiss production, perhaps since Herzog & de Meuron's insistence on the intellectual dimension of architecture in the late 1980s, has enjoyed a sense of formal variety. Projects differ as they result from divergent conceptual strategies, borne out of the reading of distinct situations. What connects the works in one architect's oeuvre is, explicitly, the architect's intellectual position, with emphasis on the role of concepts to harness and control formal impulses.

The architecture of Jonathan Woolf sets itself apart through the extent to which it is a literary, rather than strictly conceptual, enterprise. The departure point is almost always a pragmatic rehearsal of programme, means and site constraints. A discussion of what is appropriate ensues touching on issues of ordinariness, type and image. And yet, between these initial stages and the end result the creative process is more difficult to map. The resulting formal, material and tectonic expression indicate a sensitivity that goes beyond the normatively architectural. It is this sensitivity that I call literary, and this paper attempts to elucidate the meaning of this expression.

In a statement about his own work, Woolf once quoted the words of British playwright Tom Stoppard: "I begin by writing and themes come to the surface through the act of writing, not the other way around. It is therefore through beginning with perhaps a observation or a character, that the play

---

* *Irina Davidovici* is an architect and writer based in London, where she teaches history and theory of architecture at Kingston University. Her doctoral dissertation from the University of Cambridge, on Northern Swiss architecture between 1980-2000, has received the RIBA award for Outstanding PhD Thesis in 2009 and is currently being prepared for publication.

Ziel, Fragen nach Aussergewöhnlichkeit oder Angepasstheit, nach der Art und dem Aussehen oder Auftreten des architektonischen Projekts zu klären. Der kreative Prozess, der zwischen diesen Anfangsstufen und dem Endergebnis stattfindet, ist allerdings nur schwierig aufzuzeigen und nachzuvollziehen. Der hieraus resultierende formale und tektonische Ausdruck sowie die Frage nach den zu verwendenden Materialien zeugen von einer Sensibilität, die weit über das Normativ-Architektonische hinausgeht. Es ist genau diese Sensibilität, die mir von literarischer Qualität zu sein scheint und die ich in den vorliegenden Ausführungen näher beleuchten möchte.

In einem Kommentar über seine eigenen Arbeiten hat Woolf einmal die Worte des britischen Dramatikers Tom Stoppard zitiert: «Ich fange an zu schreiben und während ich schreibe entstehen die Themen und kommen an die Oberfläche – und zwar durch den Akt des Schreibens und nicht etwa umgekehrt. Ein Stück entsteht daher zu Beginn sehr langsam, vielleicht durch eine Beobachtung oder eine Figur. Es ist nicht so, dass ich zu Beginn entscheide, was das Thema des Stücks sein wird.»[1] Dieser Kommentar ist in zweifacher Hinsicht von Bedeutung. Erstens gibt er Zeugnis von der Dunkelheit und Nichtnachvollziehbarkeit des kreativ-künstlerischen Prozesses, über den auch der Künstler selbst keine vollständige Kontrolle hat. Zweitens und in unserem Zusammenhang vielleicht noch nützlicher weist dieser Kommentar auf einen Reifungsprozess hin, der jenseits der Grenzen einer vorherigen Entscheidungsfindung stattfindet.

Ähnlich wie Stoppards Theaterstücke tendieren Woolfs Projekte dazu, in ihrer Einmaligkeit als künstlerisch gestaltete Werke von einem langsamen Reifungsprozess zu profitieren. Sie entstehen nicht als vollständig abgeschlossene und fertige, starre und konzeptualistische Entitäten, vielmehr entwickeln und verzweigen sie sich durch Gespräche und Diskussionen mit Kunden, durch Neubewertungen der Projektzwänge und -beschränkungen sowie durch eine dauernde Neuinterpretation der Auftragsvorgaben. Die Wünsche und das Feedback der Kunden sind für den Entwurfsprozess von wesentlicher Bedeutung, da der architektonische Charakter des Projekts nicht zuletzt auch stark von deren Implementierung abhängt. Der literarische Aspekt der Woolfschen Architektur tritt vollends zutage, wenn man an diese Fähigkeit zur Reflektion der Umstände und Bedingungen denkt sowie an deren Vermögen, Verborgenem architektonisch Ausdruck zu verleihen.

Die Projekte, die in dieser kurzen Monographie erörtert werden, lassen sich grob in drei verschiedene Kategorien einteilen: Wettbewerb, Wohnungen, Pavillon. Bei den Wohnprojekten tritt der literarische Charakter am deutlichsten hervor, daher möchte ich diese weiter unten ein wenig ausführlicher be-

1

slowly comes into being. It is not that I decide at the beginning what the theme of the play will be."[1] This statement is useful in two ways. Firstly it testifies to the ultimate opacity of the creative process, over which the artist himself is unable to exercise full control. Secondly, more helpfully perhaps, it also indicates the existence of a maturation process, also situated beyond the limits of predetermined decision-making.

Similarly to Stoppard's plays, Woolf's projects tend towards one-off crafted pieces that benefit from a slow process of maturation. Rather than emerging as complete but rigid conceptual entities, they develop and branch out through discussions with clients, re-assessment of constraints, constant reinterpretation of the brief. The client requirements and feedback are central to the design process, to the extent that architectural character is a consequence of their implementation. The literary aspect of Woolf's architecture becomes most obvious in this ability to reflect on its circumstances, and give architectural expression to issues that otherwise tend to remain hidden.

The projects in the present monograph could be seen to fall roughly in three categories: competition, residential and pavilion. Of these, the residential projects are those whose literary character is most explicit, and these I will address in more detail below. The two competition projects, for extensions to Stockholm City Library and the Rapperswil Uni-

[1] Zitiert nach Jonathan Woolf: «Two Rooms», Vortrag während der Architecture Foundation Exhibition, St James London 1995

[1] Quoted in Jonathan Woolf, "Two Rooms", paper given at Architecture Foundation Exhibition, St James London 1995

7

handeln. Bei den beiden Wettbewerbsprojekten handelt es sich um Erweiterungen der Stockholmer Stadtbibliothek und der Erweiterung des Universitätscampus im Schweizerischen Rapperswil, also um wirklich grosse Projekte, die – da nicht gebaut – zwangsläufig etwas abstrakter ausfallen. Das Stockholmer Projekt galt der Erkundung eines nordischen Dorizismus und kombinierte zu diesem Zweck Elemente von Asplunds urbaner Formalität mit Lewerentzes Ideen zur Bedeutung des Materials. Rapperswils atmosphärische Gestaltung und Ausführung erinnern trotz Woolfs kultureller und geografischer Distanz an die Szene der Analogen Architektur in der Schweiz. Beide Projekte sind Versionen desselben Szenarios: Ohne sich auf Kollisionskurs mit der Realität zu begeben und konfrontiert mit den konkreten Problemen bei einem Projekt dieser Grössenordnung, scheinen diese beiden Entwürfe eher von einer begrifflich-konzeptualistisch geprägten Disziplin zu leben als durch narrative Details zu glänzen.

Der Monkey-Puzzle-Pavillon im schottischen Aberdeen (der nach einem aus Chile importierten Baum, der so genannten Schuppentanne, benannt wurde) steht dank der wenigen normativen Auftragsvorgaben auf halber Strecke zwischen den beiden Polen des

versity respectively, are large-scale and – as unbuilt – inescapably more abstract. The Stockholm project is guided by the study of Nordic Doricism, combining something of Asplunds' urban formality with Lewerentz' approach to material. Rapperswil's atmospheric renderings are reminiscent of the Analoge Architektur studio, despite Woolf's cultural and geographic distance from the analogue scene. Both projects are versions of the same scenario: without the head-on collision with reality and with concrete issues of scale, they seem dictated by conceptual discipline rather than narrative detail.

The monkey-puzzle pavilion in Aberdeen (named after a local tree imported from Chile) is placed, thanks to its non-prescriptive brief, halfway between the conceptual and the literary. The requirement was here for a 'meeting place', a crossroads information point for an architectural festival in the Scottish market town. Woolf's recognition of the pavilion's temporary nature and the general brief led to a move both original and ruthlessly efficient. Rather than expend energy on determining the shelter's shape and dimensions, the architect proposed the appropriation of an existing form, both architecturally recognizable and sufficiently general

2 3

Begrifflich-Konzeptualistischen und des Literarischen. Zu den Anforderungen gehörte es hier, für ein Architekturfestival einen ‚Treffpunkt' zu schaffen, einen Infopunkt am Scheideweg sozusagen. Woolf erkannte die temporäre Natur eines derartigen Pavillons und entwarf – auch dank sehr allgemeiner Auftragsvorgaben – ein äusserst ursprünglich wirkendes und gleichzeitig unbarmherzig effizientes Projekt. Statt Energie auf Gestalt und Grösse dieses Gebäudes zu verwenden, hat der Architekt eine bereits vorhandene Form vorgeschlagen, die sowohl architektonisch erkennbar als auch hinreichend allgemein war, um in diesen neuen Kontext zu passen. Ein früher Entwurf zeigte eine Kopie des Front Members' Room in der Londoner Architectural Association, der noch um eine Schornsteinsäule erweitert wurde. Das Endresultat war dann aber doch deutlich kreuzförmiger und entsprach modellhaft der Gangzone im Herzen von Valerio Olgiatis bekannter Schule in Paspels (1996-1998). Wie auch die Erschliessungszone in seinem bekannten Referenzgebäude ist der Pavillon ein Treffpunkt mit einem dezidiert städtisch-urbanen Charakter, der in diesem neuen Kontext dennoch an Aberdeens mittelalterliche Strassenanordnung erinnert.

Das zweite Projekt, das als Pavillon klassifiziert werden könnte – die Dacherweiterung und der damit verbundene Dachausbau eines bestehenden und vollständig sanierten Gebäudes in Kings Cross – ist Teil einer erforschend-abwägenden Entwicklung und daher hinsichtlich seiner formalen Konfiguration ziemlich allgemein. Das zu einem grossen Teil durch Planungszwänge und -vorgaben bestimmte Gebäude ist durch die Besonderheit seiner Öffnungen gekennzeichnet – durch viereckige Fenster mit Ausblicken über London sowie durch ein Oberlicht im Zentrum des Entwurfs. Das literarische «Momentum» offenbart sich unerwartet in Form der unzureichenden vertikalen Ausrichtung der Fenstermodule, denn die Fensterbankhöhen werden durch unterschiedliche Faktoren und Umstände der Strassenfassade und der Terrasse bestimmt. Die Unregelmässigkeit einer solchen Antwort auf externe Umstände und Faktoren liegt jenseits der klaren Disziplin formaler Prinzipien.

Das Literarische der Woolfschen Architektur tritt besonders bei den Wohnprojekten von Woolf zutage – jenen Projekten, die für eine ganz besondere Familiensituation konzipiert sind. Wie bei der Auftragsmalerei von Porträts reflektieren auch die Gebäude zu einem Teil den Charakter ihrer Besitzer, ob diese das nun bewusst wünschen oder nicht. Es ist nahezu unmöglich, in dem Zusammen- und Getrenntsein der zwei Wohnhäuser der beiden Brüder bei dem Projekt Brick Leaf House nicht etwas von deren persönlichem Verhältnis mit zu lesen. Von zentraler Bedeutung in diesem Zusammenhang ist die vertikale Akzentuierung des Schattens,

4

to fit in the new context. An early scheme figured a positive cast of the Front Members' Room in the Architectural Association, to scale and complete with chimney shaft. The final result is a more specific cruciform volume – a positive, straightened out version of the lobby space at the heart of Valerio Olgiati's well-known school in Paspels (1996–1998). Like its acknowledged reference, the pavilion offers a place of encounter that has a distinct urban character, reminiscent in its new context of Aberdeen's medieval street pattern.

The second project that could be classified as pavilion – the roof extension to an existing, fully refurbished building in Kings Cross – is part of a speculative development and thus quite general in its formal configuration. The volume, largely determined by planning constraints, is fixed in its

1. Stadtbibliothek Stockholm Luftaufnahme
2. Monkey Puzzle Pavillon
3. Der Pavillon versetzt in die Landschaft bei Aberdeen
4. Brick Leaf House Zufahrt
5. Painted House Innenansicht

1. Stockholm City Library aerial view
2. Monkey Puzzle Pavillon
3. The pavilion relocated in the Aberdonian landscape
4. Brick Leaf House driveway
5. Painted House interior

der vom Eingang des Hauses her sichtbar ist und die Trennung zwischen den zwei Wohneinheiten auf der durchgehenden Fassade andeutet (diese Einkerbung beherbergt den Hauseingang des älteren Bruders). Dieser vertikale Akzent wird im Innern durch den die Häuser trennenden Lichtschacht ergänzt, der dafür sorgt, dass das gemeinsame Schwimmbad im Untergeschoss des Gebäudes Tageslicht erhält.

Auch Pocket House antwortet mit seiner Trennung zwischen einem «kühl» wirkenden Erdgeschoss und dem «warm» wirkenden oberen Teil des Hauses sowie dem restaurierten Tonnengewölbe bedachtsam auf eine vorgefundene Situation. Zur Strategie gehörte es, statt der Zusammengehörigkeit der beiden Geschosse deren unterschiedlichen Charakter hervorzuheben und damit den vorgefundenen Stand der Dinge deutlich herauszuarbeiten. Auch bei dem Entwurf zu den Lion Rooms handelt es sich um einen mit erforschend-abwägendem Charakter, der das Gebäude und sein Umfeld einer neuen Nutzung – zu Wohnzwecken – zuführt und sich dabei an den Räumen des bereits bestehenden Gebäudes orientiert. Die zwei hier entstandenen Wohnungen behalten trotz ihrer Einheitlichkeit in Material und Details ihre jeweilige eigenständige Persönlichkeit – geradezu wie zwei Soldaten auf Urlaub – mit jeweils gleicher Uniform, aber einem jeweils individuellen Selbst.

Gegenstand des Projekts Painted House war die Umwandlung von zwei Doppelhaushälften aus den vierziger Jahren in ein grosses Doppelhaus für nur eine Familie, was einem Kommentar Woolfs zum typischen Vorortwohnen gleichkam. Während die Vorderfassade einerseits an die typischen Vorortdoppelhaushälften erinnert, zeigt sie andererseits durch ihre abstrakten Details und ihr Material doch eine unübliche Formalität. Hinter der eher typischen Fassade wurde die ungewöhnliche Innengestaltung pragmatisch an die nicht herkömmlichen, aber sehr traditionellen Bedürfnisse einer Grossfamilie von elf Personen angepasst.

Tektonisch ist das Projekt ein kompliziertes Spiel mit Materialstärken. Der Name ist als Reaktion auf die typische Innenraumgestaltung in den Vorortwohnhäusern mit ihren vielen verschiedenen Oberflächenschichten schützenden oder dekorativen Charakters zu sehen. Hier sind die Oberflächen im Inneren des Hauses im Gegensatz zu den typischen Teppichlagen, Parkettböden und Nippes-Ansammlungen nackt und bloss. Ähnlich wie Robert Venturi (Vanna Venturi House, 1962) beschwört Woolf mit diesem Projekt einen vertraut-familiären Ton, legt dabei jedoch die Essenz des Vorortwohnens bloss: Unterschied und Trennung von konventioneller Fassade und privatem Innenraum.

Der literarische Charakter dieser Projekte manifestiert sich auf verschiedene Weise. Erstens er-

place by the specificity of openings, square windows framing London views and a skylight at the centre of the deep plan. The literary moment occurs unexpectedly with the vertical misalignment of the window modules, their sill height determined by different conditions on the street façade and to the terrace. It is the irregularity of this response to external conditions that goes beyond the clear-cut discipline of formal reason.

The literary at the heart of Woolf's architecture emerges most vividly in his residential architecture – in those projects crafted around a particular family situation. Like commissioned portraits, these buildings begin to reflect something of their owners' characters, be it something they would wish or not to represent. It is difficult not to read, in the togetherness and separation of the two homes for two brothers in Brick Leaf House, something of their personal relation. A crucial moment is the strong vertical accent of shadow, visible from the access to the house, that announces on the continuous wall surface the distinction between the two residential units (this indentation houses the older brother's house entrance). The vertical accent is balanced internally by the shaft separating the houses in section, and which brings light to the shared swimming pool in the basement.

The Pocket House, with its distinction between a materially 'cold' ground floor and 'warm' upper part of the house – topped by an restored barrel-vault – also carefully responds to the found situation. The strategy, rather than unify the two floors, was to emphasise their difference of character, creating an intensification of the found state of affairs. The Lion Rooms, a speculative development changing the premises' use from commercial to residential, also takes as a departure point the range of spatial characters in the existing building. The resulting two flats, despite their consistency in materiality and detailing, retain their distinct personality – like two soldiers on leave, in identical uniform yet thoroughly themselves.

Painted House, the conversion of two 1940s semi-detached units into one family home, offers an ambivalent commentary to its suburban location. While the contour of the front façade appeals to the public subconscious to reliably signify 'suburban semi', through its abstract detailing and materiality the frontage acquires a strange formal quality. Behind the almost-ordinary façade the unusual internal organisation is pragmatically suited to the unconventional, but ultimately traditional, co-habitation of an extended family of eleven.

The project's tectonic concern is with linings, with an intricate play on the thickness – or rather, thinness – of materials. The name is, manifestly, a reaction against the conventional suburban interior, with its layering of surfaces for protection or display.

5

möglicht die langsam-behutsame, aber zunehmende Zusammenarbeit zwischen Architekt und Kunde, dass die Pläne in nahezu narrativer Art die individuellen Besonderheiten der jeweiligen Familiensituation reflektieren. Zweitens – und dies ist ein eher architektonisches Element – tritt in der tektonischen Entwicklung des Gebäudes Woolfs Originalität ungebrochen zutage. Alles geht zu Beginn der Arbeiten vom Herkömmlichen aus und wird dann an die jeweilige Situation angepasst und speziell auf die Bedürfnisse der Besitzer bzw. Bewohner des Gebäudes zugeschnitten. Drittens werden Konfiguration und Anordnung von Fenstern und Oberlichtern wie bei der Beleuchtung im Theater minutiös kontrolliert, um so Ergebnisse zu erzielen, die das Gewöhnliche transzendieren. Es gibt punktuelle Lichteffekte oder gänzlich durchflutete Lichträume, die Augenhöhe ist dabei kein massgebliches Kriterium, und das Sichtfeld wird so manipuliert, dass sich unerwartete Beziehungen zwischen den Räumlichkeiten und deren Bewohnern offenbaren.

Die Offenheit und das Spielerische der Woolfschen Architektur erinnern an Rossis Satz von der «ehrlichen Unordnung der Dinge» – universale Fragen werden durch genaustens auf das Besondere abgestimmte Antworten thematisiert. Die literarische Sensibilität dieser Arbeiten ist letztlich das Ergebnis ihrer Kombination aus Verstand, kreativem Geist und Esprit, der Fähigkeit zur freien Assoziierung, aus der unerwartete Beziehungen hervorgehen. Dies ist gleichbedeutend mit der Bildung von Metaphern.

The internal surfaces are laid bare in contrast to the expected profusion of carpets, parquet and knick-knacks. Similar to Robert Venturi (Vanna Venturi House, 1962), Woolf appeals in this project to a dimension of familiarity while exposing the essence of suburbia: the disjunction between a conventional façade and the private interior.

The literary character of these projects manifests itself in several ways. Firstly, a slow and growing collaborative process between architect and client allows the plan and section to reveal the particulars of each family situation in an almost narrative fashion. Secondly, and more strictly architectural, is the buildings' tectonic development, in which Woolf's discrete originality is given full rein. Detailing starts from the conventional and is developed according to each situation, with the buildings effectively tailored around their occupiers' needs and desires. Thirdly, the configuration and placement of windows and skylights is theatrically controlled to achieve results that transcend the ordinary. Light bounces or penetrates, the eye level is frustrated, and the field of vision manipulated to reveal unexpected relations between spaces and, by extension, their inhabitants.

The openness and playfulness of Woolf's architecture recalls what Rossi once called the "honest disorder of things" – it addresses universal concerns through finely tuned responses to the particular. The literary sensitivity of this work is ultimately a consequence of its wit, the capacity to create unexpected associations, which is another definition for the creation of metaphors.

Painted House, Golders Green, London
2009
mit Bharat Patel

Zwei für die Zwischenkriegszeit typische Doppelhaushälften in einem Nordlondoner Vorort wurden in ein grosses Doppelhaus für eine erweiterte Familie von elf Personen umgebaut.

Die Woolf-Architekten interessieren sich seit einiger Zeit für die britische Tendenz, bei der die Konstruktionsstärken immer geringer werden, gleichzeitig aber ihre Oberflächeneigenschaften behalten werden. Zur selben Zeit haben wir uns auch mit der Farbe als Material und dem Anstrich beschäftigt. Dies ist kein neues Phänomen. Im georgianischen England wurde ebenfalls akribisch mit Farbe gearbeitet, um völlig verschiedene Atmosphären zu schaffen, die jeweils gänzlich unterschiedliche Materialien mit einer einzigen «all over» Oberflächenbehandlung zusammenfügten. In diesem Haus wurden nahezu sämtliche Innenoberflächen, Wände, Decken, Böden und auch alle Tischlerarbeiten gestrichen oder mit einer Deckschicht versehen, um sie farblich zusammen zu führen. Dies gibt den herkömmlich gestalteten Räumen einen abstrakten Charakter.

Der Umbau respektiert die bereits vorhandenen Raumstrukturen, die im hinteren Teil und an den Seiten des Grundstücks frühzeitig erweitert wurden. Sie werden bis auf zwei Etagen durch das neue Projekt herausgearbeitet und mit einem bewohnbaren Loft unter einem neuen Dach ergänzt. Im Erdgeschoss wurde ein Stahlrahmen eingebaut, der grosszügig proportionierte gemeinsame Wohnräume schafft und die Grösse der erweiterten Familiewohneinheit reflektiert. Es sind Erholungs- und Arbeitszimmer für die Kinder, eine grosse Küche sowie ein Ess- und Wohnbereich mit grossen Schiebetüren, die sich zum hinteren Garten hin öffnen lassen.

Painted House, Golders Green, London
2009
with Bharat Patel

Two typical inter-war semis in a north London suburb have been converted into a large double house for an extended family of eleven people.
Woolf Architects have been interested for some time in the way that UK construction methods rely on materials that are becoming thinner and thinner whilst at the same time striving to retain their surface material qualities. At the same time they have been studying paint as a material in and of itself. This is not a new phenomenon. The Georgians used paint meticulously to define a range of atmospheres that united several different materials within an 'over-all' (or 'all over') finish. In this house almost all of the interior surfaces, walls, ceiling, floors and joinery are either painted or laminated to match paint. This lends the conventional shaped volumes an abstract character.

The new building works within the footprint of the existing properties, both of which had been extended previously on one level both at the rear and sides of the plot. The new project extrudes these up to two floors together with an inhabited loft within a new roof shell. A steel frame has been inserted at ground level to achieve generous proportioned social spaces on the ground floor, which are of a scale in keeping with the size of this extended family unit, and include recreation and study spaces for the children, a large kitchen, eating and living area with large sliding windows opening onto the rear garden.

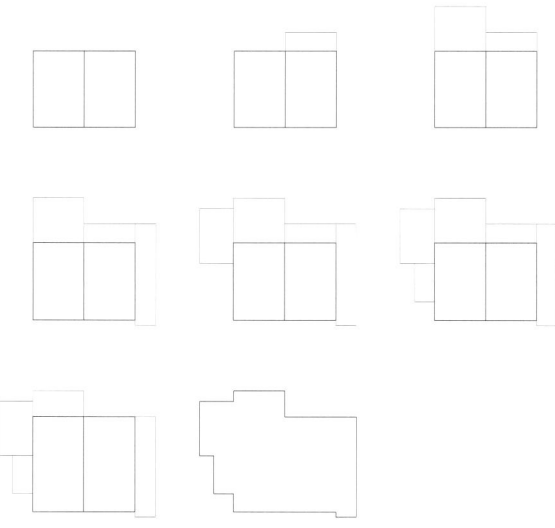

1 2 3

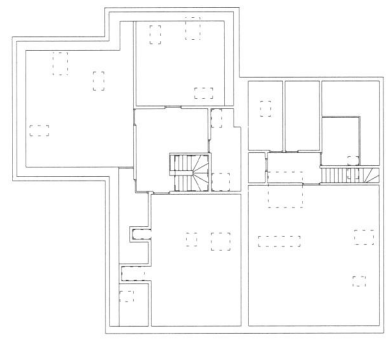

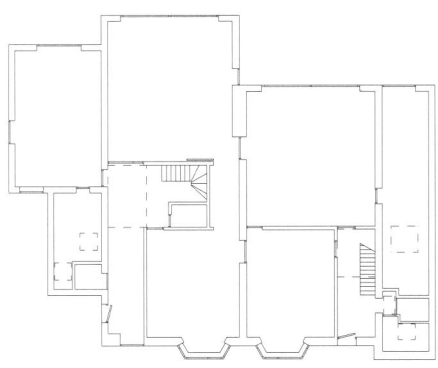

1. Modell
2. Grundriss-Diagramme in verschiedenen Stadien
3. Vorderfassade
4. Grundriss des zweiten Geschosses 1:400
5. Grundriss des ersten Geschosses 1:400
6. Grundriss des Erdgeschosses 1:400
7. Flur im Erdgeschoss
8. Küche
9. Spielzimmer/Fitnessraum im zweiten Geschoss
10. Innenansicht Erdgeschoss

1. model
2. plan evolution
3. front facade
4. 2nd floor plan 1:400
5. 1st floor plan 1:400
6. ground floor plan 1:400
7. ground floor hallway
8. kitchen
9. 2nd floor playroom/exercise room
10. ground floor interior

Stockholmer Stadtbibliothek
Wettbewerb 2007

Stockholm City Library
Competition 2007

Das Projekt ist das Ergebnis eines Wettbewerbs zur Erweiterung von Gunnar Asplunds ikonischer Stadtbibliothek von 1932 im Stadtzentrum von Stockholm. Im Wettbewerb ist der Abriss von vier bestehenden Annexgebäuden und die Bereitstellung einer zusätzlichen Bibliotheksfläche von 30 000 m² vorgegeben. Der Hauptteil der neuen Bibliothek ist in einem siebenstöckigen «Bücherlagerhaus» untergebracht, das als Gegenstück zu Asplunds Bibliotheksgebäude fungiert. Das neue Gebäude steht in respektvollem Abstand am anderen Ende des Geländes und widerspiegelt die Geometrie des Originals, wird dabei aber auch seiner urbanen Bedeutung gerecht, da es sich in die Strukturen der angrenzenden Bürotürme aus den 60er Jahren einpasst und selbige auf diese Weise in ein Ensemble integriert. Der Eingang zur neuen Bibliothek erfolgt über eine lange, langsam ansteigende Platte, an deren Ende ein Café und die 24 Stunden geöffnete Bibliothek liegen. Der Hügel mit dem Observatorium ragt über diese weiträumige Platte hinaus und wird damit Bestandteil eines neuen Bibliotheksgartens und einer Fussgängerroute ins Stadtzentrum von Stockholm.

Das neue Gebäude reinterpretiert die Raum-nach-Raum-Museumstypologie der ursprünglichen Bibliothek als Etage-auf-Etage-Version, wobei keine Etage der anderen gleicht. Dies wurde durch zeitgenössische Neuinterpretationen redundanter Industriegebäude inspiriert, wo innerhalb des ganzen Blocks auf separaten Etagen verschiedenste Firmen oder Büro- bzw. Wohneinheiten angesiedelt sind, so dass sich hinter jeder Tür eine neue Umgebung oder Tätigkeit entdecken lässt. Dieses Konzept entspricht dem Kundenwunsch nach einer grossen, neuen Bibliothek, die in eine Abfolge thematisch angeordneter Etagen unterteilt werden kann, so dass jede dieser Etagen unabhängig von den anderen gestaltet und genutzt werden kann. Das Projekt erhielt die Auszeichnung «Honorary Mention», da es beim internationalen Wettbewerb mit 1170 Bewerberprojekten unter die ersten zehn gelangte. Für diesen Ort wurde noch kein Projekt endgültig beschlossen.

The project is a competition to extend Gunnar Asplund's 1932 iconic city library in the centre of Stockholm. The brief called for the removal of four existing annex buildings and the provision of 30,000 m² of additional library space.

The bulk of the library is housed within a seven-storey 'warehouse of books' acting as a counterpoint to Asplund's library building. The new building sits at a respectful distance towards the far end of the site, it's geometry aligning with the original but it's urban role is also to rhyme with the adjacent 1960's office towers, giving them a new role as part of an ensemble. The new library is entered through a long low slanting plinth that forms an entrance with a 24hr library and cafe. The Observatory hill laps onto this plinth, forming a new library garden and pedestrian route into the city centre.

The new building reinterprets the room-to-room museum typology of the original library as a floor-to-floor experience, and no two floors are the same. This is partly inspired by the contemporary reinterpretations of redundant industrial buildings where a number of businesses or dwellings occupy separate floors within the whole, so that a new environment or activity can be discovered behind each doorway. This approach addresses the client's desire for the large new library to be divided into a sequence of themed floors, each of which could be curated and operate independently of the others. The project received an Honorary Mention for reaching the last ten in international competition that attracted 1,170 entries. No project has yet been agreed for the site.

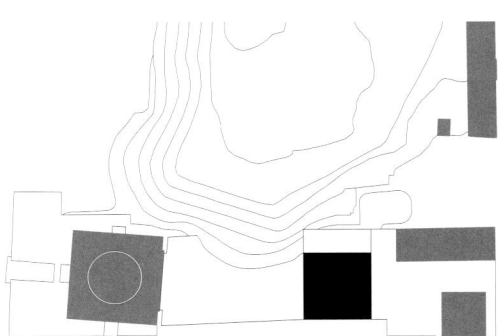

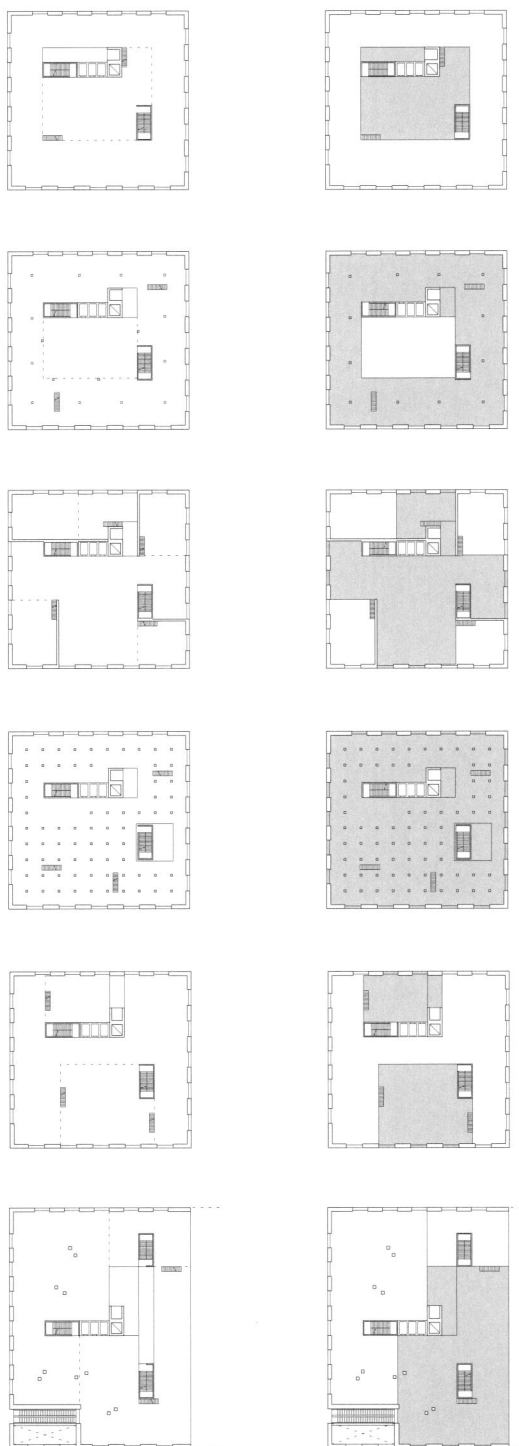
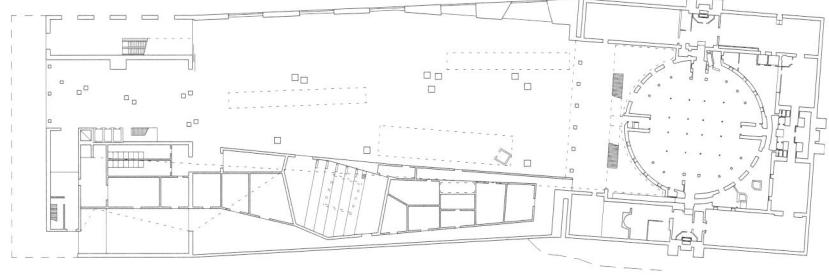

1. Lageplan 1:4000
2. Blick von Asplunds Bibliothek aus
3. Grundrisse des ersten bis zum sechsten Geschoss mit Mezzaninen 1:1500
4. Grundriss des Erdgeschosses 1: 1500
5. Innenansicht des Forums
6. Schnitt des Forums 1:1500
7. Längsschnitt der Bibliothek 1:1500
8. Haupterhebung 1:1500
9. Innenansicht des Lesesaals

1. site plan 1:4000
2. view from Asplund's library
3. 1st to 6th floor plans with mezzanines 1:1500
4. ground floor plan 1: 1500
5. forum interior
6. short section through forum 1:1500
7. long section through library 1:1500
8. main elevation 1:1500
9. reading room interior

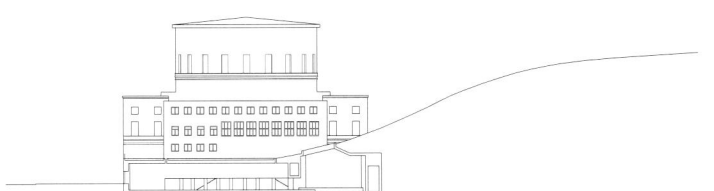
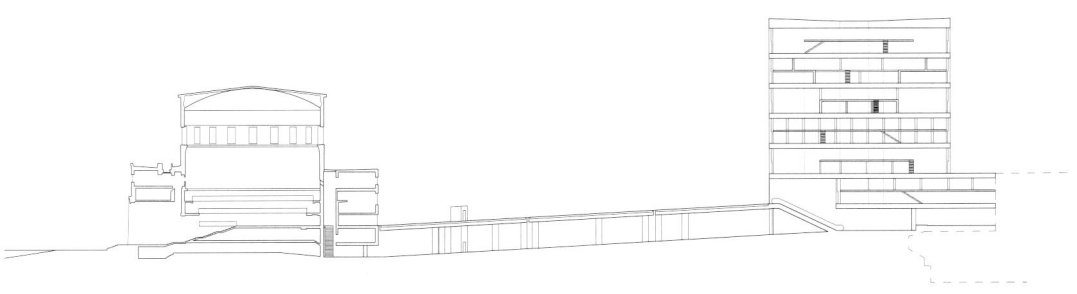

22

6
7
8 9

Brick Leaf House, Hampstead, London
2003

Das Gebäude befindet sich am Rande von Hampstead Heath, einer stellenweise ländlichen Heidelandschaft im Norden Londons. Laut Auftrag sollte ein Zweifamilienhaus von 1000 m² Wohnfläche auf einem Grundstück von 3000 m² erstellt werden. Zum Bauprogramm zählen zwei voneinander unabhängige Wohn- und Unterhaltungsbereiche mit jeweils eigenem Zugang sowie ein gemeinsames Schwimmbad mit Fitnessraum unter den Häusern.

Das Grundstück fällt von vorn bis hinten über neun Meter ab und wird von zwei alten Bäumen dominiert, einer sehr grossen Blutbuche und einer Stieleiche. Das Gebäude ist etwa gleichhoch wie die beiden Bäume, dient als verbindendes Element zwischen diesen, definiert einen unteren und einen oberen Gartenbereich. Die Häuser stehen Rücken an Rücken und zeichnen sich durch eine am Aussenbereich orientierte Raumanordnung um einen durch ein Oberlicht mittig beleuchteten Raum aus. Jedes dieser Atrien ist mit einem per Computer automatisierten Schiebeglasdach ausgestattet, das es ermöglicht, die Räume bei Sonnenschein so weit zu öffnen, dass sie wie offene Hofräume anmuten und das Gebäude auf natürliche Weise belüften.

Die Idee, zwei Wohneinheiten in einer einzigen Form miteinander zu verbinden, wurde in England zu Beginn des 20. Jahrhunderts – in Form der Doppelhaushälften – in den Vororten etabliert. Aber auch die frühere Tradition eines vornehmen Hauses für die erweiterte Familie kannte das Wohnen mehrerer Familienmitglieder unter einem Dach, etwa in den Venetovillen von Andrea Palladio, die von Brüdern bewohnt wurden. Mit der Verbindung von zwei eigenständigen Teilen in einer einzigen Form erhält Brick Leaf House ein vornehmes Ambiente, das zur Umgebung passt, ohne dass dabei Bau- und Materialkosten in ungeahnte Höhen schiessen.

Brick Leaf House, Hampstead, London
2003

The building is located on one of the edges of Hampstead Heath, a semi rural woodland in north London. The brief asks for a two family residence of 1000 m² within a 3000 m² plot. The residence includes two independently accessed living/entertaining areas and a communal swimming pool with gym beneath the houses.

The plot slopes over 9m from front to back and is dominated by two mature trees, a giant copper beach and an English oak. The building is similar in scale to the trees and is set between them as a linking element defining a lower and upper garden. The houses are organised back-to-back and rely on a simple configuration of outward facing rooms around a top lit circulation space lighting the centre of the plan. Each of these atria has an all glass sliding roof, computer controlled to open during sunshine hours, thus transforming the spaces into external courts and naturally ventilating the building.

The idea to join two dwellings into a single form was established in England in the early 20's with the suburban semi-detached house. However, the earlier tradition of a grand house for the extended family also tended to include several members of the same family, as was the case with Andrea Palladio's Veneto Villas which were time shared between brothers. With Brick Leaf house, the strategy of a single form composed of two discreet parts creates a sense of grandeur appropriate to the location without resort to an overly expensive constructional and material treatment.

1   2   3

1. Modell
2. Lageplan 1:4000
3. Zufahrt
4. Detail der Ostfassade
5. Ansicht der Südfassade
6. Grundriss oberes erstes Geschoss und Dachaufsicht 1:400
7. Grundriss Hochparterre und unteres erstes Geschoss 1:400
8. Grundriss Keller und Untergeschoss 1:400
9. Oberes Atrium
10. Innenansicht des Untergeschosses
11. Längsschnitt
12. Zimmer im unteren ersten Geschoss
13. Schwimmbad

1. site model
2. site plan 1:4000
3. driveway
4. east facade detail
5. view of south facade
6. upper 1st floor and roof plan 1:400
7. upper ground floor and lower 1st floor plan 1:400
8. basement and lower ground floor plan 1:400
9. view of upper atrium
10. lower ground floor interior
11. long section
12. lower first floor bedroom
13. pool

4	6
5	7
	8

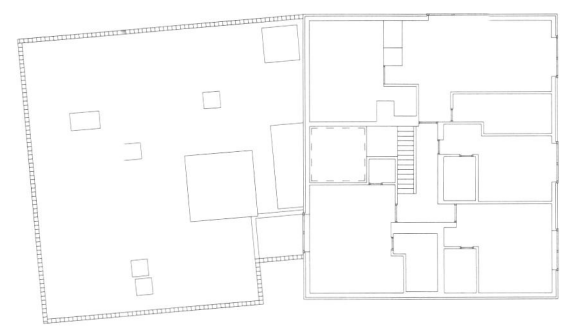

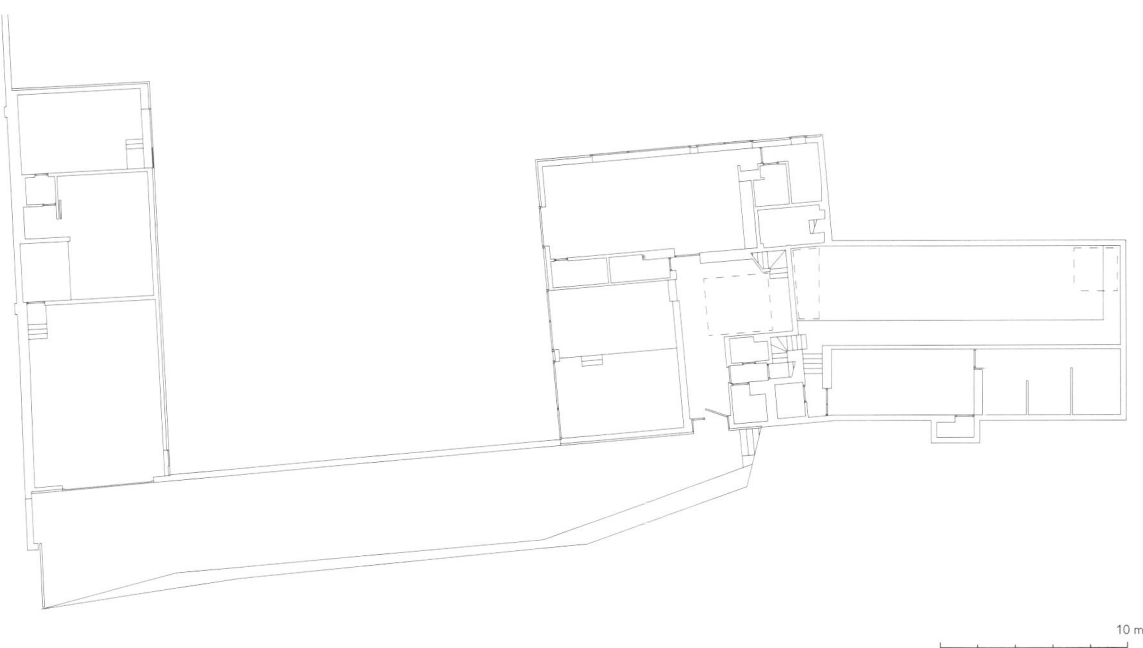

27

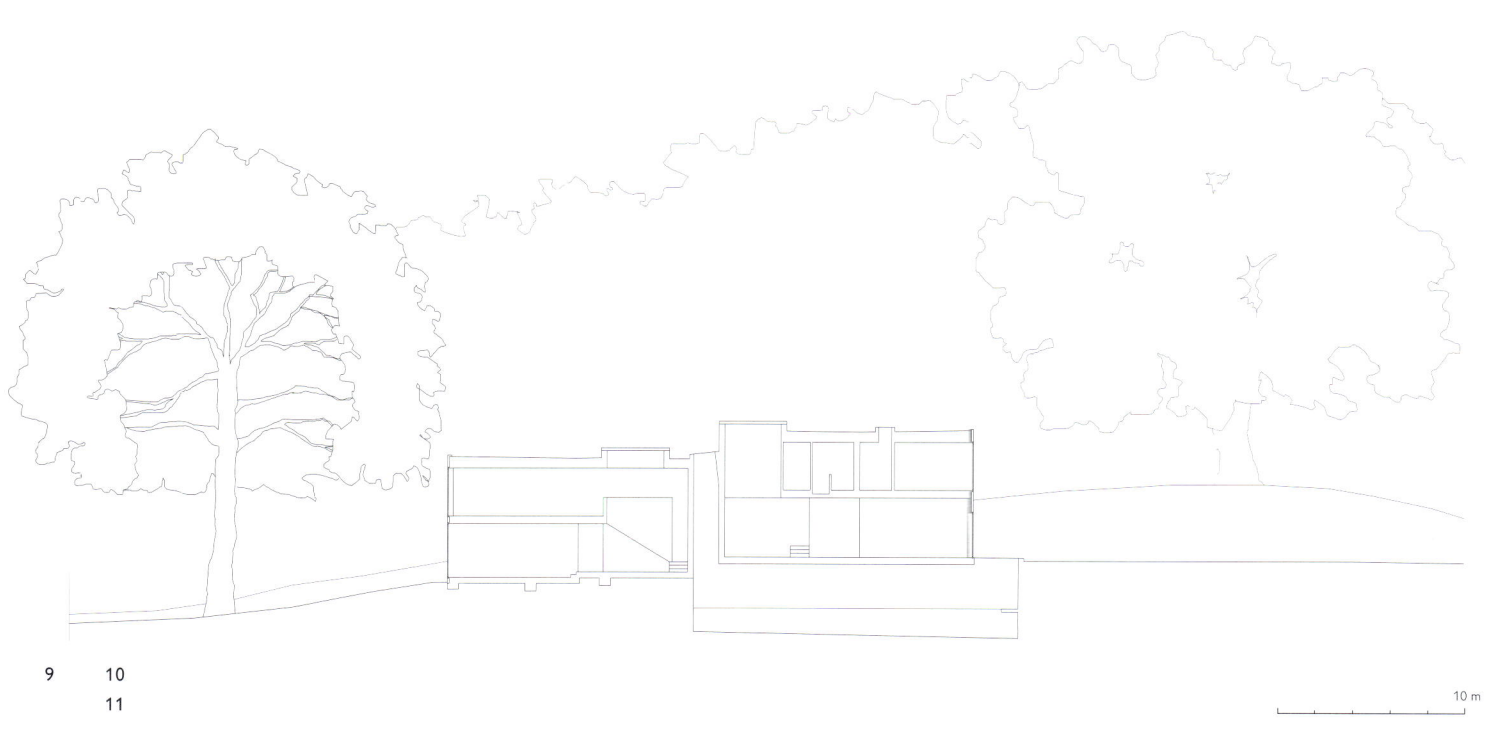

9
10
11

10 m

29

12 13

Monkey Puzzle Pavillon, Aberdeen
2007

Ein Pavillon ist ein ephemeres Stück Architektur, an das keine grossen Ansprüche gestellt wird und dessen Lebenserwartung in der Regel recht kurz ausfällt. Anschliessend wird das Gebäude abgerissen und das Stück Land wieder der Natur zurückgegeben. In dieser Hinsicht entspricht es daher mehr der Abstraktion eines echten Gebäudes und ist eher mit Produktdesign vergleichbar.

Der Monkey Puzzle Pavillon wurde als zentrale Anlaufstelle für das Six Cities Design Festival im Herzen der schottischen Stadt Aberdeen konzipiert und diente während dieser Zeit als Informations-, Ausstellungs- und Veranstaltungszentrum, als «Mikrokino» und allgemeiner Treffpunkt.

Das Gebäude ist eine Art Kreuz- oder Übergangspunkt, an dem Wege ineinander führen und Richtungen eingeschlagen werden, es dient aber auch als ein Portal oder Gateway. Seine Grundform wurde durch einen Teil eines sehr bekannten Gebäudes des Architekten Valerio Olgiati in den Schweizer Alpen von Graubünden inspiriert und es ist in etwa so gross wie ein Aberdeener Bungalow. Seine merkwürdige Form erinnert an ein deformiertes oder verschobenes Kreuz. Alle Arme des Kreuzes sind verschieden gross und bieten eine Reihe von Räumen mit einem Fenster oder einem Durchgang, von denen man in die verschiedenen Himmelsrichtungen blicken kann. In der Mitte des Pavillons befindet sich ein Fenster zum Himmel.

Das Gebäude und sein Dach bestehen innen wie aussen aus Grobspanplatten, so genannten OSB-Platten. Holzschnitzel, die mit einem speziellen Kleber unter Druck zu festen Platten zusammengepresst werden. Sie weisen eine Oberflächenstruktur auf, die an fossilienähnliche Muster und damit trotz seiner industriellen Herstellung an ein Naturprodukt erinnert.

Monkey Puzzle Pavilion, Aberdeen
2007

A pavilion is an ephemeral piece of architecture, with an undemanding and usually short life span, following which the building is taken down and the land it sits on returned to nature. In this respect it is an abstract of a proper building, perhaps more like a piece of product design.

The Monkey Puzzle Pavilion was commissioned as a centrepiece for the city of Aberdeen's contribution to the Six Cities Design Festival, and during that time functioned as an exhibition and event venue, a cinema and meeting place.

The building can be thought of as a crossing point, where paths meet and directions are taken, but also like a portal or gateway. Drawn from a fragment of a famous building by the architect Valerio Olgiati in the Swiss mountains of Graubunden and more or less the same size as an Aberdonian bungalow, it's a strange shape for a building, being like a deformed or stretched cross. Each arm of the cross is a different size offering a range of spaces and either a window or doorway that can look to the points of the compass. In the centre a window to the sky.

The building comprises sheets of 'oriented strand board', inside and out on walls and on the roof. Made from shavings of wood, compressed with glue to make a rigid board, the surface is rich in its 'fossilised' pattern, clearly recognisable as being from nature even though it's industrial.

1 2

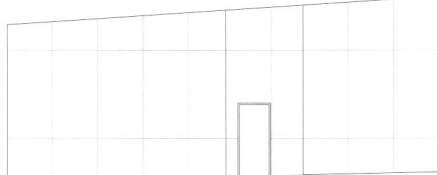
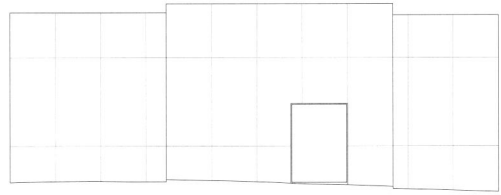
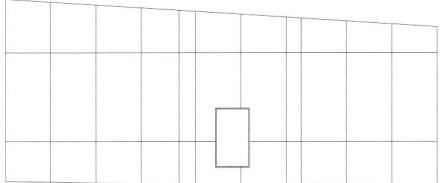
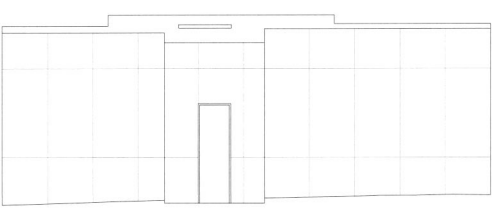
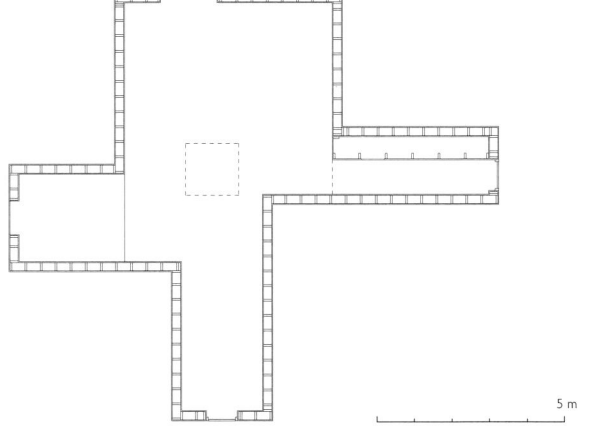

1. Modell
2. Blick über den Platz
3. Ansichten 1:200
4. Grundriss 1:200
5. Detail im Innern
6. Innenansicht
7. Innenansicht
8. Ansicht von Norden

1. model
2. view across the square
3. elevations 1:200
4. plan 1:200
5. interior detail
6. interior
7. interior
8. view from the north

3 5
4 6

7   8

Pocket House, Notting Hill, London
2000

Das Pocket House mit seiner schmalen Vorderfront, einer Tür und nur einem Fenster zur Strasse hinaus liegt am Ende einer Sackgasse. Es wirkt neben den angrenzenden Regency-Häusern sehr klein. Das im 19. Jahrhundert gebaute Haus war ehemals ein Künstleratelier. Das Gebäude verfügt über zwei Etagen, ein grosszügiges und helles Obergeschoss und ein niedrigeres Erdgeschoss, das unter Terrain liegt und so eine deutlich kühlere, ausgeglichene Temperatur aufweist. Mit dem Projekt wird dieser Gegensatz durch die Auswahl von Baumaterialien und Oberflächenbehandlungen – die entweder warm und weich oder kühl und glatt sind – entsprechend in Szene gesetzt.

Die Räume im Obergeschoss bleiben erhalten. Unterhalb und seitlich des Hauptraumes entstehen neue, ergänzende Räume. Von der schmalen Strassenfront her gelangt man durch einen kleinen Vorraum in den Hauptraum, der mit einem grosszügigen Tonnengewölbe überdeckt ist. An seiner Stirnseite sieht man in einen ummauerten Hofgarten. Im Gewölbe ist ein breites Dachfenster eingeschnitten und zwei Öffnungen führen zu weiteren Räumen.

Zum ersten Mal wird bei diesem Projekt das Interesse auf die «vierwandige» Raumgestaltung gelenkt und dieses Prinzip auch konsequent auf jeden Bereich des Hauses angewendet. Jedem Raum, auch dem Eingangsbereich, dem Treppenhaus, der Küche und dem Arbeitszimmer, wird der Status eines eigenständigen Raumes mit vier Wänden zugestanden. Allerdings wird die klassische Form eines geschlossenen Raums in einem gewissen Mass durch die verschiedenartigen und unterschiedlich grossen Schwellen zwischen den Räumen abgewandelt.

Pocket House, Notting Hill, London
2000

Dwarfed by the grand late regency houses either side of it, Pocket House is at the end of a cul de sac, with a tiny frontage of just a door and one window. The house was formerly an artists studio built in the 19th century. The building offers two floors, an upper tall and well lit space above a lower floor formed within primarily earth retaining walls and thus providing a markedly cooler controlled temperature. The project focuses this contrast by selecting constructional and finishing materials that are either warm and soft or cool and polished.

The project restores the formal shape of the upper floor and adds other rooms below and beside the main space. The tiny street presence leads via a small lobby into the main space, a generous barrel-vaulted room looking onto a walled garden at one end, a large rooflight above, and two openings leading to other rooms.

The project is the first to develop interest in room making and apply it rigorously to each part of the house. Each space, whether an entrance, a staircase, a kitchen or a study, is given the status of a four-walled room, but the classical sense of enclosure is to some extent thwarted by varying the size and nature of thresholds between them.

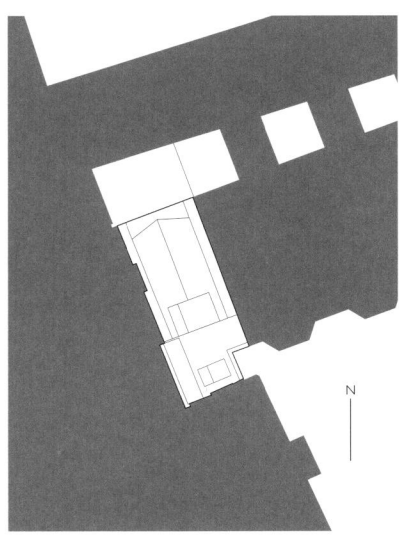

1 2 3

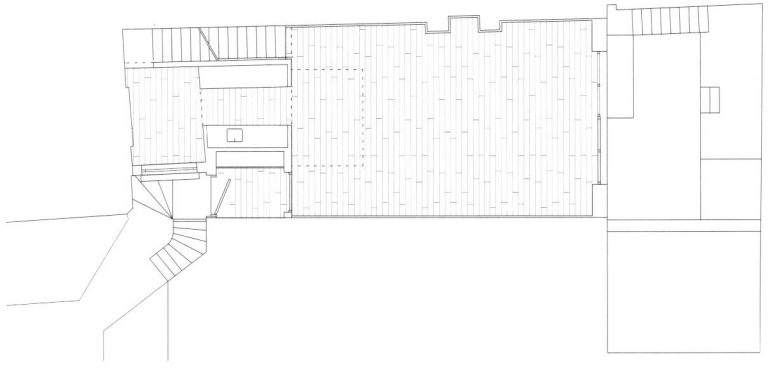

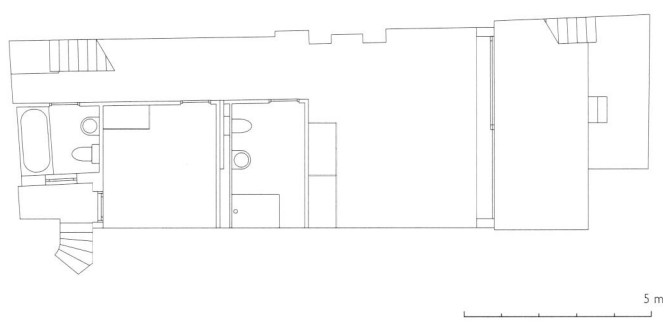

5 m

1. Schnittmodell
2. Lageplan 1:500
3. Innenansicht des Hauptraums
4. Grundriss Erdgeschoss 1:200
5. Grundriss Untergeschoss 1:200
6. Ansicht der Rückseite 1:200
7. Schnitt 1: 200
8. Detail im Aussenbereich
9. Detail im Untergeschoss
10. Innenansicht Untergeschoss
11. Treppe zum ersten Stock

1. sectional model
2. site plan 1:500
3. main room interior
4. ground floor plan 1:200
5. lower ground floor plan 1:200
6. rear elevation 1:200
7. section 1: 200
8. exterior detail
9. lower ground interior detail
10. lower ground interior
11. stairs to first floor

Universitätsgebäude Rapperswil
Wettbewerb 2007

Rapperswil University Buildings
Competition 2007

Dieses Projekt ist als Ergänzung des Universitäts-Campus angelegt und zeigt, wie ein derartiger Eingriff die unmittelbare Umgebung und die ganze Stadt selbst beeinflussen kann. Es sollten ein neues Fakultätsgebäude, Studentenwohnheime sowie eine Rahmenstruktur für zukünftige Gebäude geschaffen werden. Der Eingriff reflektiert seine Rolle und Bedeutung als Ergänzung der Seepromenade. Er bewahrt deren Qualität als einer Reihe von offenen Räumen, die sich dem Ufer entlang entfalten und Teil einer weiträumigen Landschaft sind, die sich um den See herum erstreckt.

Die Bauvolumen gestalten die Randbereiche dieses Ortes. An den entferntesten Stellen werden sie unter Bezugnahme auf den städtischen Kontext gross und hoch, während sie in der Nähe der Wohnsiedlungen klein und niedrig bleiben und den gebotenen Respekt walten lassen. Die Universität wird an die Stadt angebunden und die Bedeutung und vornehme Grosszügigkeit des Ortes werden erneut akzentuiert. Die neuen Gebäude betonen die Übergänge der Geometrie des bestehenden Campusgeländes (mit Bezug zum Seeufer gestaltet) zu den übrigen Gebäuden am See (im rechten Winkel zum Ufer gesetzt).

Die Holzgebäude sind aus vorgefertigten Elementen, die abhängig von der Funktion des Gebäudes in Tonalität und Arrangement variieren. Holz wurde auf Grund des Verhältnisses zur natürlichen Umgebung und wegen seines würdevollen Alterns – wie es auch den bestehenden Korten-Stahlgebäuden eigen ist – ausgewählt. Das Konstruktionssystem unterstreicht den Charakter der Holzkonstruktion aus Säulen und Balken, die grosszügige Durchgänge zu den Räumen im Innern ermöglichen.

This project, for additions to a university campus, is aware of how an intervention like this can impact both on its immediate surroundings and on the city itself. The programme asked for a new faculty building, housing for students and a framework plan for future additional buildings. The proposal carefully considers its role in completing the lakeside promenade and maintains the existing situation of a series of informal open spaces along the shore, forming part of a large-scale landscape that engages the lakeside.

The project designs the edges of the site. It grows high on the furthest points in relation to the city landscape and becomes low and respectful when close to existing buildings. It links the university to the city, and re-establishes the grandness and importance of the location. The new buildings hinge the transition in geometry from that of the campus (originally designed to relate to the lakeside) to that of the other buildings along the lake (perpendicular to the shore).

The proposed timber buildings are based on a family of prefabricated components that vary in tonality and arrangement in relation to the function of the building. Timber has been chosen for its relationship with the natural surroundings of the site and for its ability to age gracefully in a similar fashion to the 'Corten' steel campus buildings. The construction system provides the buildings with a character that expresses timber construction, columns and beams that create generous openings to the rooms inside.

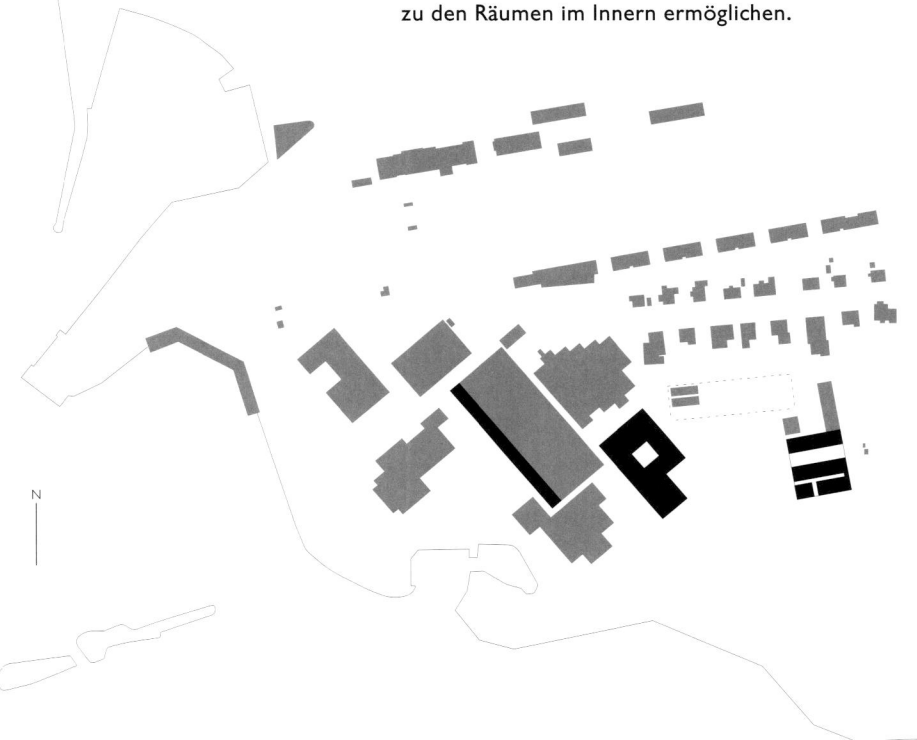

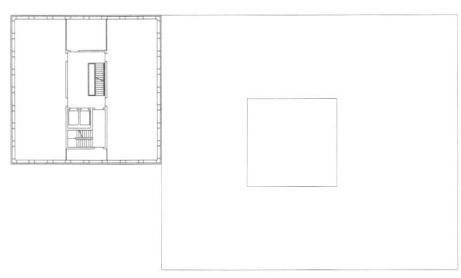

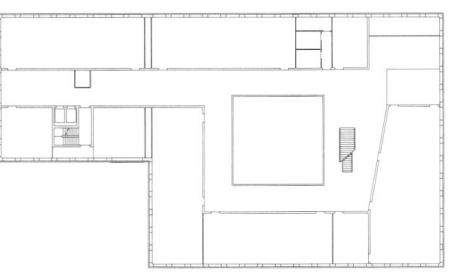

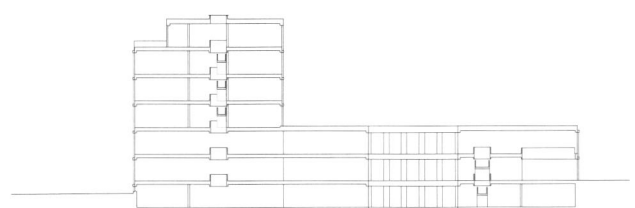

1. Lageplan 1:5000
2. Ansicht des Forschungszentrums
3. Grundriss zweites Geschoss 1:1000
4. Grundriss Erdgeschoss 1:1000
5. Längsschnitt 1:1000
6. Blick vom See
7. Innenansicht im Erdgeschosses

1. site plan 1:5000
2. exterior view of research centre
3. 2nd floor plan 1:1000
4. ground floor plan 1:1000
5. long section 1:1000
6. view from the lake
7. ground floor interior

The Lion Rooms, Islington, London
2003

Dieses Gebäude ist eines von vier um 1850 gebauten ehemaligen Pubs. Hier war bis in die 40er Jahre des 20. Jahrhunderts der grösste Viehmarkt von ganz Europa, auf den über den Bahnhof Kings Cross Vieh von überall in England zum Verkauf gebracht wurde. Das vornehme Aussehen dieser italianisierenden viktorianischen Gebäude unterstrich deren Bedeutung als Handelsplatz und Hotelanlage für die reicheren Viehbesitzer.

Im Erd- und Kellergeschoss werden zwei Wohn- und Arbeitseinheiten eingebaut. Die klassische Art, Räume hintereinander anzuordnen, sorgt nicht nur für eine individuelle Privatsphäre für mehrere Bewohner, sondern auch für individuelle Gestaltungsmöglichkeiten und eine je eigene Atmosphäre. Würde derselbe Bereich im Stil eines Loft gestaltet, wäre die Ausübung verschiedener Tätigkeiten zur gleichen Zeit unmöglich, da alles zu jeder Zeit einsehbar bleibt und der Raum nicht abhängig von seiner jeweiligen Nutzung geöffnet oder geschlossen werden kann. Eine Reihe von neuen seitlichen Höfen, die ihrer Form nach den Innenräumen entsprechen und zur Beleuchtung der früheren Kellerräume dienen, werten alle Räume auf. Jede Einheit verfügt über einen Zugang durch den eigenen Hof. Die räumliche Veränderung des bestehenden Erdgeschosses ist dank der alten Eisenrahmenkonstruktion möglich, auch wenn die Hierarchie der verschiedenen Pub-Bereiche weiterhin les- und sichtbar ist. Im Inneren bleibt die architektonische Sprache stumm und verstärkt damit die Wirkung der vorhandenen verzierten Räume des Gebäudes. Dort wo sich die Innenbereiche bis in die Höfe erstrecken, werden die vorhandenen Fassadenpilaster zu Wandteilen der Innenräume.

The Lion Rooms, Islington, London
2003

The building is one of four former pubs built in 1850 and that marked the corner of what, until the 1940's, was the largest cattle market in Europe where animals from all over England would be driven up from Kings Cross station. The grand scale of these Italianate Victorian buildings signified their importance both as the place where deals would be struck and as hotels for the wealthier cattle owners.

The project converts ground and basement floors into two suites for living and working. This classical way of arranging rooms together in sequence provides not just for individual privacy of several occupants, but offer each its own atmosphere. The same space opened up 'loft' style is unable to promote different activities at the same time, everything remains on show all the time, and space does not open and close with the flow of use.

The strategy is enhanced with a series of new courtyard spaces that are room-like in form and extended down to light the former cellars. Each unit is entered via it's own courtyard. The spatial expansiveness of the existing ground floor is the result of the old iron frame structure, though the hierarchy of different pub areas is still legible. Internally the language is mute, illuminating the power of the existing building's decorated rooms, and where the interior extends into former yards, the exterior pilastery is brought inside.

1 2

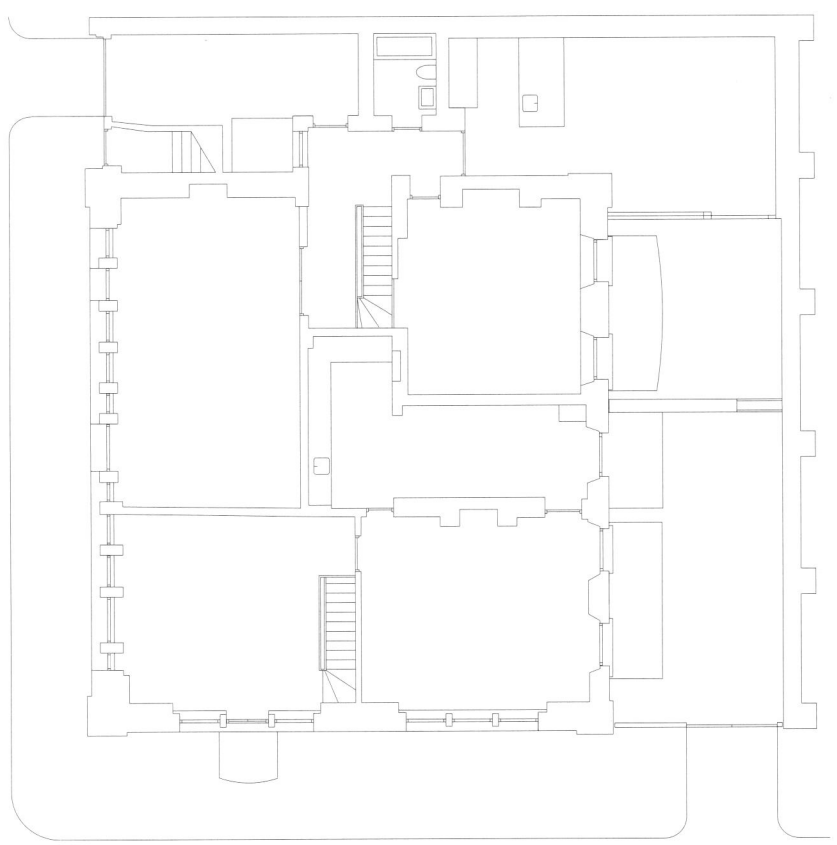

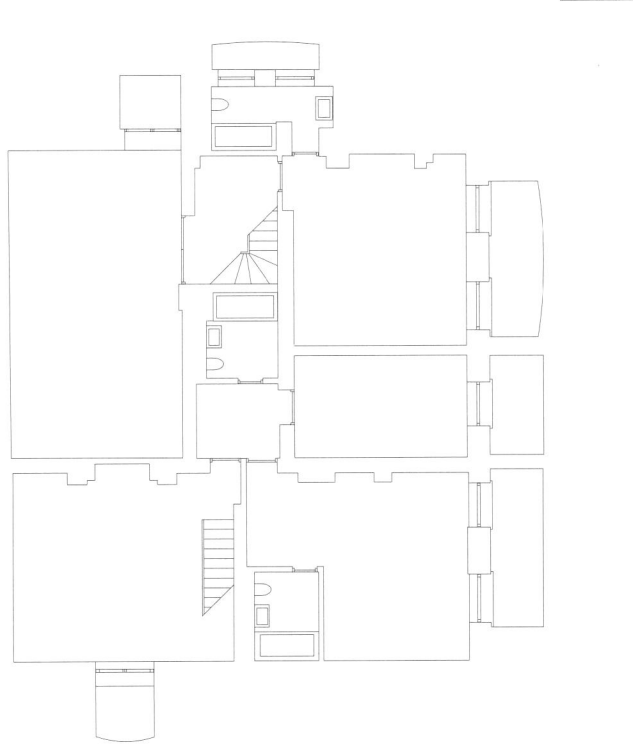

1. Aussenansicht
2. Innenansicht Erdgeschoss
3. Grundriss Erdgeschoss 1:200
4. Grundriss Untergeschoss 1:200
5. Innenansicht Erdgeschoss
6. Innenansicht Erdgeschoss und Hof

1. exterior view
2. ground floor interior
3. ground floor plan 1:200
4. lower ground floor plan 1:200
5. ground floor interior
6. ground floor interior and courtyard

Swinton Street Studios, Kings Cross, London
2001

Das Büro wurde 1998 durch einen Wettbewerb zur Ausführung des ersten von mehreren Projekten des Londoner Bauträgers Heights UK Ltd. ausgewählt. Das Gebäude markiert den Rand des ersten offenen Tunnels der U-Bahn-Linie Metropolitan Underground, die in den 50er Jahren des 19. Jahrhunderts gebaut wurde. Als dieser Tunnel das rechtwinkelige Strassenraster des 18. Jahrhunderts diagonal durchschnitt, wurden die Restparzellen sofort zu kommerziellen Zwecken bebaut und genutzt. Die trapezförmigen Grundflächen entstanden aus den beiden Geometrien.

Das bestehende Gebäude wurde ursprünglich zur Reparatur der Pferdewagen und Kutschen genutzt, die in einen offenen Hofraum entweder vor oder hinter dem Gebäude gezogen wurden.

Tragende Backsteinwände umschliessen den Hof und sie sind auch im Hofinnern eingesetzt, so dass das Gebäude die Formplastizität einer Arbeit von Alvaro Siza besitzt. In dieses Lagergebäude aus Backstein werden Holzrahmenwände eingezogen, die der neuen Nutzung auf jeder Etage entsprechen. Im Dachaufbau werden die trapezförmigen Strukturen des Gebäudes in kleinerem Massstab wiederholt. Es ist eine Holzrahmenkonstruktion mit einer Aussenhaut aus wiederverwertetem Dachschiefer. Die Erweiterung des Gebäudes zeichnet sich durch ein in jeder Fassade wiederholtes Fenstermodul aus. Die vertikale Position des Fensters wird vom Querschnitt des alten Gebäudes bestimmt.

Swinton Street Studios, Kings Cross, London
2001

In 1998 the office was selected through competition to carry out the first of several projects with the London property developer Heights UK Ltd. The building forms the edge of the first open tunnel for the Metropolitan Underground tube line built in the 1850's. When this tunnel cut diagonally across the 18th century orthogonal street grid, the immediate parcels of left over land were built for commercial uses, each representing the trapezoidal space resulting from the two geometries.

This particular building was originally used for the repair of the horse drawn carriages, the 'cabs' being hoisted up an open yard and into the either the front or back of the building.

Faced entirely from load bearing brick wrapping both around and into the courtyard the building has the plasticity of form of a work by Alvaro Siza. Into this brick warehouse building are placed timber frame walls that define the new domestic brief on each floor. The roof addition is a scaled down repeat of the trapezium building below. It is a timber frame structure clad in salvaged roofing slates. This extension of the building has a repeated window module to each façade, their varying heights determined by the old buildings profile.

1 2

1. Planmodelle
2. Ansicht von Norden
3. Treppenhaus
4. Innenansicht Arbeitszimmer im Obergeschoss
5. Küche

1. models of plan arrangement
2. view from the north
3. staircase
4. top floor studio interior
5. kitchen

    4
3   5

Werkverzeichnis/List of Works
Auswahl Bauten, Projekte und Wettbewerbe/Selection of Buildings, Projects and Competitions

1991	01	Ijaz apartment, London
	02	Dublin Urban Regeneration, Ireland. Competition, 1st prize. Collaborators: Renato Benedetti, Jonathan McDowell
	03	Office of the Future, Milan. Competition, 1st prize. Collaborator: Harvey Langston-Jones
1992	04	Bath Room, London. Competition
	05	Bicycle House, London
1993	06	Glass Cottage, London
	07	Piano House, London
	08	Ziggurat Studio 1, London
1994	09	Fellner Dellal House, London
1995	10	Narrow House, London
	11	Hulme Housing, Manchester. Competition
	12	DB Studio 1, London
	13	Wood Lights, London. Product. Competition

01 02
03 05

1997	14	Photographer's Studio, London
	15	DB Studio 2, London
	16	Sculptor's House, London
1998	17	East Molesey Housing, Surrey, Competition. Collaborator: Juan Salgado
	18	Devereux House-Hotel, Channel Islands. Project
	19	Car Museum, Essex. Project
	20	Hidden Apartment, Amsterdam, NL. Project
	21	Cocoon, Europe. Project. Collaborator: Petra Blaisse
	22	Blue Marlin Offices, Bath. Collaborator: Juan Salgado
	23	Adolfo Dominguez Store, Manchester. Collaborator: Juan Salgado
	24	Ziggurat Studio2, London
	25	Amsterdam Regeneration, NL. Competition. Collaborator: Juan Salgado
2000	26	Pocket House, London
	27	Queens Gate Place Mews, London

07 13
15 18

2001	28	Swinton Street Studios, London.
	29	Kitchen, London. Product
2003	30	End House, London. Project
	31	The Lion Rooms, London
	32	Brick Leaf House, London
	33	Hat House, London. Project
	34	York Way Apartments, London
2004	35	Highgate Hill House, London. Project
	36	Newlyn Art Gallery, Cornwall. Competition
	37	House and the City, Aberdeen/London. Installation
2005	38	Town House, London. Project
	39	Yentob House, London
	40	Giant's Causeway Interpretation Centre, Northern Ireland. Competition

34   37
40   41

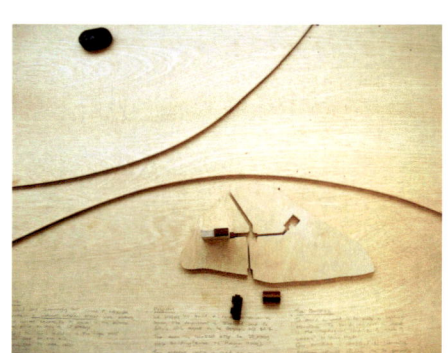

	41	Olympics Pavilion, Stratford, London. Competition
	42	A Table Chair, London. Product
2006	43	Lootch Moscow, Russia. Competition
	44	Mayfair Offices, London
2007	45	Mayfair Penthouses, London
	46	Monkey Puzzle Pavilion, Aberdeen, Scotland
	47	Dublin Public Library, Ireland. Competition
	48	Beulah Road, London
	49	Bath Country House, Bath. Competition
	50	Rapperswil University Buildings, Switzerland. Competition
	51	Mount Pleasant, London. Students of L'accademia di Mendrisio, Diego Calderon, Annabarbara Suter
	52	Stockholm City Library, Sweden Competition, shortlisted

44 49
50 51

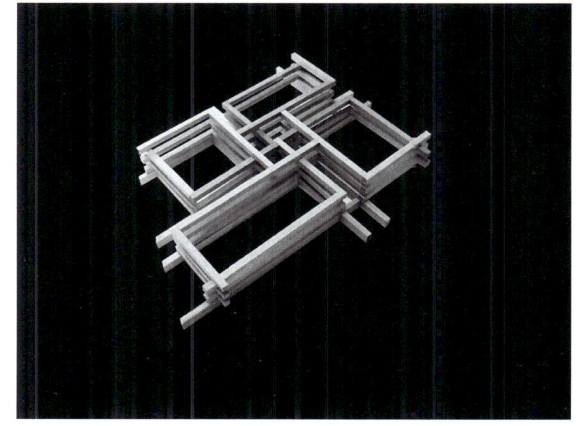

2008	53	Bloomsbury Apartments, London. Project
	54	Museum of Ethnography, Geneva, Switzerland. Competition
2009	55	Painted House, London. Collaborator: Bharat Patel

Laufende Projekte/Current projects:
56   Holland Park House, London
57   101 House, London
58   House on a hillside, Nairobi, Kenya
59   Three houses in a garden, Nairobi, Kenya

55	57
58	59

Jonathan Woolf	1961	geboren in London
	1979–1988	BA-Abschluss (Honours) und Architekturdiplom an der Kingston School of Architecture, London (Tutoren: John Farmer, David Dunster, Werner Kreis, Brendan Woods)
	1982–1984	Praktika und Mitarbeit bei Vallefuoco Brauer in Rom, Adams Falla Associates und Douglas Paskin Asscciates in London
	1987–1990	Praktikum und Mitarbeit bei Munkenbeck and Marshall Architects, London; Mitglied des RIBA als eingetragener Architek; Projektarchitekt für das Haus von Charles Saatchi in Chelsea, London
	1990	Gründung von Jonathan Woolf Architects
	1995–1998	Lehrer an der Architectural Association, London (Intermediate-School-Unit)
	1995–1998	Co-Referent an der Universität Bath bei David Shalev (OBE; Diploma-School-Year)
	2003	Auszeichnung für Brick Leaf House
	2004	Publikation: A New English House
	2003–2007	Professor für Architektur an der Robert Gordon University in Aberdeen (Schottland)
	2007–2009	Gastprofessor an der Accademia di Architettura in Mendrisio (Schweiz)
	1961	Born in London
	1979–1988	Ba honours degree and diploma in architecture at Kingston School of Architecture Tutors John Farmer, David Dunster, Werner Kreis and Brendan Woods
	1982–1984	Apprenticed with Vallefuoco Brauer, Rome, Adams Falla Associates, and Douglas Paskin Associates, London
	1987–1990	Apprenticed with Munkenbeck and Marshall Architects, London. Joined RIBA as Chartered Architect. Project architect for the house of Charles Saatchi, Chelsea, London.
	1990	Established Jonathan Woolf Architects
	1995–1998	Intermediate School Unit Master at the Architectural Association, London
	1995–1998	Diploma year master at the University of Bath, with David Shalev OBE
	2003	Completion of award winning Brick Leaf House
	2004	Publication of 'A New English House'
	2003–2007	Professor of architecture at the Robert Gordon University, Aberdeen UK
	2007–2009	Visiting Professor at L'Accademia di Architettura di Mendrisio CH

MitarbeiterInnen/Collaborators Aktuelles Team; Stand 2010/ Current team; status 2010	Ben Wright, Carlos Sanchez, Diego Calderon; Mirjam Nymalm, Tom Benton, Thomas Goodey, Simon Davisor, Claire Curtice
Frühere MitarbeiterInnen/ Former collaborators	Christopher Snow (1995–06), Andrew Phillips (1992–95), Jonathan Sergison (1993) Xenia Adjoubei, Medine Altiok, Roi Carrera, Doug Carson, Tim Collett, Stuart Coughlin, Irina Davidovici, Mattia Donati, Olivia Fauvelle, Verena Hoch, Harvey Langston-Jones, Fawn Ma, Simone Mantel, Laurent Pereira, Ben Perman, Moa Rundlof, Susan Russell, Tomoaki Saito, Emilie Schickel, Marcin Skolimowski, Ulrich Stockhaus, Annabarbara Suter, Sei Takenaka, Ursula Vielhaber, Andy Wakefield, Cheryl Wigger, Christine Wohlrab, Carlo Zucchia

Postskriptum
Valerio Olgiati

Die Gespräche zwischen Jonathan Woolf und mir drehen sich eher um Ideen und nicht um Erfahrungen. Wir versuchen, Dinge zu denken, nicht einander Dinge zu erzählen. Darum sind wir befreundet.
Als Architekt ist Jonathan Woolf in der urbanen Tradition der eleganten, geistvollen und ruhigen englischen Architektur verwurzelt, und dennoch zeichnet sich sein Oeuvre durch eine kraftvolle Dialektik aus.
Ich habe mir seine beiden Arbeiten *Brick Leaf House* und *Painted House* angesehen. Sie oszillieren zwischen Anonymität und vornehm-kultivierter Raffinesse. Es sind zwei wirklich sehr gelungene architektonische Arbeiten.
In der neuen zurückhaltenden englischen Bewegung einer eigentlich «unsichtbaren Architektur» ist Jonathan wohl der einfallsreichste und klügste Kopf. Er steht für das, was ich unter Englischer Kultiviertheit verstehe.

Postscript
Valerio Olgiati

With Jonathan Woolf I have conversations that are based more on ideas than on experience. It's about generating things and less about telling each other things. This is why we are friends.
As an architect he is rooted in the urban tradition of elegant and calm English architecture, but nevertheless his oeuvre is characterized by a vigorous dialectic.
I have visited his *Brick Leaf House* and his *Painted House*. They oscillate between anonymity and refinement. Two very beautiful pieces of architecture.
In the distinguished new English movement of "invisible architecture" Jonathan is the sharpest and most spirited one. He stands for what I understand as English sophistication.

Quart Verlag Luzern/Quart Publishers Lucerne

De aedibus international
5 Tony Fretton Architects (dt/e)
4 Jonathan Woolf Architects (dt/e)
3 Hufnagel Pütz Rafaelian (dt/e)
2 Hild und K (dt/e)
1 Stanton Williams (dt/e)

De aedibus – Zeitgenössische Architekten und ihre Bauten/Contemporary architects and their buildings
36 Schneider & Schneider (dt/e)
35 Frei & Ehrensperger (dt und e)
34 Liechti Graf Zumsteg (dt/e)
33 Adrian Streich (dt/e)
32 Daniele Marques (dt/e)
31 Neff Neumann (dt/e)
30 Giraudi Wettstein (dt/e)
29 Steinmann & Schmid (dt/e)
28 Matthias Ackermann (dt/e)
27 Aeby & Perneger (dt/e)
26 Bakker & Blanc (dt/e)
25 Markus Wespi Jérôme de Meuron (dt/e)
24 Bauart (dt/e und dt/f)
23 Knapkiewicz & Fickert (dt/e)
22 Marcel Ferrier (dt/e)
21 Wild Bär Architekten (dt/e)
20 Enzmann + Fischer (dt/e)
19 Mierta und Kurt Lazzarini (dt/e)
18 Rolf Mühlethaler (dt/e)
17 Pablo Horváth (dt/e)
16 Brauen + Wälchli (dt/e)
15 E2A Eckert Eckert Architekten (dt/e)
14 Lussi + Halter (dt/e)
13 Philipp Brühwiler (dt/e)
12 Scheitlin – Syfrig + Partner (dt/e)
11 Vittorio Magnago Lampugnani. Stadtarchitekturen/Urban Architectures (dt/e)
10 Bonnard Woeffray. Time (dt/e und dt/f)
9 Graber Pulver. Werkstücke/Workpieces (dt/e)
8 Burkhalter Sumi/Makiol Wiederkehr. Konstruktionen/Constructions (dt/e)
7 Gigon/Guyer. Projekte (dt und e)
6 Andrea Bassi. Figuren (dt, f und e)
5 Dieter Jüngling und Andreas Hagmann. Bauwerke (dt und e)
4 Beat Consoni. Fünf Arbeiten (dt und e)
3 Max Bosshard & Christoph Luchsinger. Abdruck Ausdruck (dt)
2 Miroslav Šik. Altneu (dt, e und i)
1 Valentin Bearth & Andrea Deplazes. Räumlinge (dt, e und i)

Monografien/Monographs
Valerio Olgiati (dt und e)
Burkard Meyer. Konkret/Concrete (dt/e)
Gion A. Caminada. Cul zuffel e l'aura dado (dt/e)

Einzelausgaben/Individual editions
Claudio Greco: Pier Luigi Nervi (dt und i)
Adrian Schiess. Farbräume. Zusammenarbeit mit den Architekten Herzog & de Meuron und Gigon/Guyer 1993–2003 (dt/e)
14 Studentenprojekte bei Valerio Olgiati 1998–2000 (dt/e/i)

Quart Verlag GmbH, Heinz Wirz; Verlag für Architektur und Kunst
Denkmalstrasse 2, CH-6006 Luzern; books@quart.ch, www.quart.ch